GALAXY OF SUPERSTARS

Leonardo DiCaprio

Hanson

LeAnn Rimes

Spice Girls

Jonathan Taylor Thomas

Venus Williams

CHELSEA HOUSE PUBLISHERS

GALAXY OF SUPERSTARS

Leonardo DiCaprio

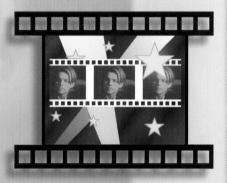

Stacey Stauffer

CHELSEA HOUSE PUBLISHERS
Philadelphia

Produced by
21st Century Publishing and Communications
a division of Tiger & Dragon International, Corp.
New York, New York
http://www.21cpc.com

Editor: Elaine Andrews
Picture Researcher: Hong Xiao
Electronic Composition and Production: Bill Kannar
Design and Art Direction: Irving S. Berman

CHELSEA HOUSE PUBLISHERS

Editor in Chief: Stephen Reginald
Managing Editor: James D. Gallagher
Production Manager: Pamela Loos
Art Director: Sara Davis
Director of Photography: Judy L. Hasday
Senior Production Editor: Lisa Chippendale
Publishing Coordinator: James McAvoy
Cover Design: Ian Varrassi/Brian Wible

Front Cover Photo: Archive Photo/Popperfoto
Back Cover Photo: Photofest

The Chelsea House World Wide Web site address is
http://www.chelseahouse.com

First Printing

1 3 5 7 9 8 6 4 2

Library of Congress Cataloging-in-Publication Data

Stauffer, Stacey, 1973-
    Leonardo DiCaprio / Stacey Stauffer.
    p. cm. – (Galaxy of superstars)
    Includes bibliographical references and index.
    Summary: A biography of the young star who has built his career
on roles in such films as "The Basketball Diaries," "Romeo and Juliet,"
and "Titanic."
    ISBN 0-7910-5151-X
    1. DiCaprio, Leonardo—Juvenile literature 2. Motion picture actors
and actresses—United States—Biography—Juvenile literature.
[1. DiCaprio, Leonardo. 2. Actors and actresses.] I.Title. II. Series.
PN2287.D4635S72 1998
791.43'028'092—dc21
[b]   98—40867
                                                                          CIP
                                                                           AC

Dedication
For Beck, Gret, Kris, "E", Pam, "D", & Shar; may we all experience L.T.E.D.C.N.S.

CONTENTS

1

"MAKING IT COUNT"

Before the ceremony even began, people tuned into their televisions waiting for his appearance. Who would he come with? As the screams began and the cameras flashed, the two appeared arm-in-arm. The most talked about and romanticized couple on the big screen had just arrived at the 55th annual Golden Globe Awards. Fans rejoiced as Leonardo DiCaprio escorted his fellow *Titanic* star, Kate Winslet, to the ceremony on Sunday, January 18, 1998. With *Titanic* holding eight nominations, including Best Actor and Best Actress, the two young stars were the talk of the evening. When reporters encountered the couple, the big question everyone wondered about was asked: "Did you two come together?" Kate smiled as her escort answered, "Yes, we came together. But we're just good buddies." Shouting fans and flashing cameras surrounded Leonardo as he made his way to the entrance of the Beverly Hilton Hotel. Once inside, cameras continued to pursue him.

Just a month before, many people would have asked, "Leonardo who?" Now, with the biggest-grossing movie ever on his resume, Leonardo DiCaprio was a name and a

---

Leonardo DiCaprio captured the hearts of adoring fans worldwide with his moving performance in the blockbuster film Titanic. *His portrayal of the heroic passenger Jack Dawson was the defining role of his career and catapulted him into superstardom.*

face that could not go unnoticed. Even amid countless superstars at one of Hollywood's most prestigious award shows, it was Leonardo who captured the attention of the audience. *Titanic's* director, James Cameron, recognized the audience enthusiasm and invited the two young stars on stage with him while accepting the Golden Globe Award for Best Dramatic Motion Picture, just one of the four Golden Globe awards that *Titanic* seized. Cameron described the duo's roles during his acceptance speech: "Leo and Kate are the center of this picture." To his fans' dismay, Leonardo did not leave that evening with the Best Actor award. Nevertheless, he walked away with as many admirers, if not more, than he had walked in with. And he would continue to be "king of the world," or at least king of the movie world, long after the hoopla of the Golden Globes was over.

During *Titanic's* filming, Leonardo hesitated to bellow the words "I'm the king of the world!" while standing at the bow of the world's most famous ship. He thought it was a corny statement, but reluctantly he shouted the line. Little did he realize that these words would go down as one of the most famous lines in movie history, or that he would become one of the most sought-after actors on the big screen. *Titanic* raised Leonardo's career status to superstardom in a matter of weeks.

The young actor did have a following, but it had not been so enormous that he could not escape his fans and enjoy life much like other people. After *Titanic* everything changed. Leonardo's handsome face appeared in scores of teen magazines and entertainment publications as well as in books and on websites.

He had begun his acting career in commercials and short-term television roles. Now he was famous for his role in the most successful movie ever. Like *Titanic*, Leonardo's popularity soared, and his wave of success continues to swell with no apparent obstacle to slow it down.

Leonardo's role in *Titanic*, that of Jack Dawson, was so different from any other part he had played that at first he was not sure he wanted to accept it. Although Jack is a wanderer, he is not troubled, insecure, or a drug addict—problems that other characters Leonardo had portrayed struggled with. Jack is a free-spirited, fun-loving guy who values the freedom with which he lives.

Leonardo finally accepted the part of the roaming artist aboard the ill-fated ship, and it proved to be a real challenge. "I've been used to playing characters that have been tortured by some sort of internal angst," he says. "It was an adjustment to play someone like this. It was a lot more challenging than I thought it would ever be. When you play someone that's sort of so vulnerable, almost like an open book in a sense, you don't have anything to fall back on as far as what he's internally going through. . . . It's a lot easier to play a tortured soul than a happy-go-lucky soul."

More than the challenging role attracted Leonardo to *Titanic*, however. "I've not done like, huge sorts of gigantic blockbuster action films simply because, to me, they've lacked content as far as the story is concerned," he explains. "But when I read and saw the script for *Titanic*, it was a completely different situation." Like director Cameron, Leonardo recognized the

Leonardo and Kate Winslet play a tense scene as Jack and Rose in Titanic. *Playing the carefree, open-hearted Jack was a departure for Leonardo, whose previous roles traditionally portrayed troubled, strung-out souls.*

deeper themes of the story, which made it so unique compared to other big-budget films. It was not just a story of a tragic event with so many lives lost. It tells of a time when people had such faith in machines and their own intelligence that they believed they could create something indestructible. It was about an era when human egos often took precedence over human feelings. Rigid class distinctions separated people, and marriages were often loveless arrangements. These themes had to be subtle enough not to be overwhelming, yet apparent enough not to only be seen but deeply felt.

What better way to do this than to present two characters, each from distinctly different classes, who help each other become more caring human beings and whose secret romance captures viewers' hearts before the couple's fate is revealed? Viewers feel the charm, the attraction and excitement, and the love expressed by the characters, and then are emotionally involved in the lovers' terror, loss, and loneliness.

One reason audiences relate so closely to Jack and his love, Rose DeWitt Bukater, is that the chemistry between Kate Winslet and Leonardo becomes apparent on screen. They thoroughly enjoyed working together and spent a lot of time goofing off whenever they could get away with it. Leonardo says about his on-set relationship with Kate: "I mean, we have it in real life. I think she's such a terrific girl. It's unbelievable. We were such good friends throughout this whole movie. . . . She's such a solid actress, and possesses so much strength on-screen, it's unbelievable. And I think she's gonna be one of our best!"

Kate also has nothing less than glowing remarks about her costar. She commented, "Leo's a natural. The actor of the century. Nobody can get near him at this point." It is ironic that at first, Cameron was not sure he wanted Leonardo to portray Jack. Once Leonardo auditioned, however, Cameron saw the young actor's undeniable charisma. He knew Leonardo was perfect for the part.

Working on the *Titanic* set was difficult for Kate and Leonardo, who had to spend what seemed like endless hours filming scenes in icy water. Their relief was a hot tub on the set they

Kate and Leonardo discuss a scene with director James Cameron on the Titanic *set. Cameron knew Leonardo was right for the part, but he made it clear that the young actor would have to follow the director's idea of Jack's character, insisting that Jack was not going to be "brooding and neurotic."*

could jump into after their many wet, chilly scenes. In addition to the strenuous physical challenge, some scenes made the young actors a little uncomfortable. On the first day, they shot the sensual scene in which Jack sketches the disrobed Rose. Leonardo was so nervous about sitting next to a nude Kate that she made a joke of it and suddenly flashed him. Kate describes another incident that day: "I was having my makeup put on—with nothing on—and there was Leo. He saw me and went 'Whooa!' and I said, 'We're going to spend the whole day like this; we might as well get over it now.' That broke the ice."

When *Titanic* was released the week before Christmas 1997, reviews were mixed. Most critics favored the movie, but some had harsh words for a film they believed was a waste of money. Audiences, however, had different ideas, being immediately swept into the excitement and magic of *Titanic*. The film brought in a whopping $28.6 million the first week of its release, and its sales remained strong enough to keep it in the top box office spot for more than 14 weeks. It went on to be the first movie to reach the billion-dollar mark and became the top-grossing film of all time.

No one could have imagined *Titanic*'s affect on viewers. Men and women, young and old, sobbed as they left theaters. Viewers could not seem to get enough of this more than three-hour epic, returning to see it again and again. The film hit a chord in audiences that seemed to compel people to talk constantly about it. As one viewer revealed to *Teen People*, ". . . I was moved to tears that seemed to never stop. I cried more in that theater than ever in my life. It wasn't just a movie but a life experience." Another fan agrees, "*Titanic* explores the reaches of love, compassion and giving to which we all aspire. How many of us could leave the theater and not say, 'Wow, I wish I had love like that?'"

Titanic's success did not stop with viewer approval. Nominated for 14 Academy Awards, and tying with *All About Eve* for the most nominations ever, the film walked away with 11 Oscars, including one for Best Picture. Leonardo was not nominated for Best Actor, however, which caused consternation among many fans. But Leonardo would have been up against industry heavyweights such as Robert Duvall, Peter Fonda, and Jack Nicholson.

Considering his youth and the direction his career is taking, Leonardo will undoubtedly have plenty of future chances to deliver an Oscar acceptance speech.

Why is it that so many movie fans, particularly women, flock to see the film more than once? One reason is Leonardo's portrayal of Jack Dawson. The young actor creates such a romantic, charming, and heroic character that women of all ages find themselves swooning over this young man.

Since *Titanic*, Leonardo has gained a popularity that surpasses that of many superstars. It is impossible to pass a newsstand on which his face does not grace the cover of a magazine or two. Bookstores have devoted whole sections to Leonardo and the scores of publications about him. Television shows that follow the stars, such as *Extra!* and *Access Hollywood*, have chronicled Leonardo's every move since *Titanic*. The public is catching up on the years of his life and career they missed out on prior to *Titanic*. Many who might have bypassed Leonardo's performances in *William Shakespeare's Romeo + Juliet*, *What's Eating Gilbert Grape*, *The Basketball Diaries*, and other films, have flocked to video stores to rent these tapes.

Titanic remained at theaters for more than half a year, and its box-office take far exceeded that of any film in history. Yet the profits will not end there. The video was released in September 1998, and sales were astronomical. Leonardo's fame is still sailing as well. He earned a reported $2.5 million for his role as Jack Dawson. It is now predicted that he will earn $20 million for future starring roles. Even

if he did not match his fellow actors with an Academy Award nomination, he was matching them and even surpassing them in the wages category. It may be hard to believe that such fame and fortune would not change someone. But his family and most of his friends contend that he is still the same old Leonardo. What is perhaps more difficult to believe is how different Leo's life is now from what it was as a child—or even just a year ago.

Leonardo, Kate, and James Cameron enjoy one of Titanic's *many awards. Although Leonardo's portrayal of Jack has been characterized as a "star-making performance," an Academy Award nomination for Best Actor eluded him—for now, that is.*

2

"Growing Up on the Other Side of Hollywood"

One day in 1974, George and Irmelin DiCaprio were strolling through the Uffuzi Museum in Florence, Italy, admiring an exhibit. Gazing at a painting by Leonardo da Vinci, Irmelin felt a hard kick in her stomach. At that moment, Irmelin decided she would name her unborn son after the famous artist, for she believed that the kick was some sort of sign. On November 11, 1974, Leonardo Wilhelm DiCaprio was born in Los Angeles. His paternal grandfather's middle name was Leon, which helped to clinch the decision for the baby's name. Leonardo's middle name is that of his maternal grandfather, Wilhelm Idenbirken.

Leonardo was born into the heart of the entertainment industry—Hollywood. His parents met in college and were still young and considerably short on money when they married, moved to Los Angeles, and had Leonardo. For most of Leonardo's first year, the family shared a perfect life, despite financial difficulties. But the pressures soon became more than the young couple could bear, and George and Irmelin eventually separated.

Even though Leonardo was barely out of infancy, he

Leonardo is not ashamed of his childhood growing up on the wrong side of the tracks in Hollywood. He credits the love and support of his parents, and their encouragement to do his own thing, in helping him overcome the less-than-glamourous environment.

does not feel he missed having a complete family. Both his parents have always played a large part in his life. In fact, Leonardo lived with his mother until he moved into his own Los Angeles home in 1997. The boy was often with his father, and the three DiCaprios gathered with one another whenever possible. Irmelin recalls, "George and I have always spent a lot of time together with Leonardo. While he was growing up, we always had dinner together and took him out to amusement parks and movies." Leonardo agrees and easily recalls the many good times he had with his parents, both together and individually.

Although he grew up in Hollywood, Leonardo did not live in the glamourous or glitzy part. "I lived in the ghettos of Hollywood. My mom thought Hollywood was the place where all the great stuff was going on. But meanwhile it was a disgusting place to be." Leo was aware of the harsh realities of Hollywood life at an early age. He saw the effects of drugs, encountered prostitutes, and even witnessed explicit sexual activities on the streets of his neighborhood.

George and Irmelin could not afford a fancy lifestyle for Leonardo. Rather, they fulfilled the child's much greater need by lavishing him with love and affection and encouraging him to express his creative side. Leonardo's mom drove him to University Elementary School in Westwood, an hour's drive from their home, just so he could receive the best education possible. "Our family wasn't exactly well off," he explains, "but I remember going to elementary school specifically because it was there that I hung out with a lot of kids that had much more money than us. I got to hang out at really fantastic homes, so while I didn't grow up with a lot of money, I grew up with that background. I was always sort of treated in the best possible way. My mother," he says proudly, "wanted to always sort of give me the best."

Although Leonardo's parents were supportive and loving, they were not the traditional mom and dad. George and Irmelin were former hippies with quite liberal views. For instance, they never excluded their son from conversations with some of their more exotic friends, even when the talk turned to sex or drugs. For many years, George earned his living creating and distributing underground comic books from his garage. George's work encouraged Leonardo's love for collecting comic books and baseball cards, and together father and son often browsed through comics and baseball cards at conventions.

Leonardo saw only one drawback to having such liberal parents. He never had anything new to try that would surprise them. There was nothing to rebel against, as he said. "Whatever I did would be something they'd already done. I mean, my dad would welcome it if I got a nose ring!"

Leonardo's mother also gave her son further opportunities for creative freedom. Irmelin often took the boy to Germany, her birthplace and the home of her parents. Leonardo's grandparents adored him, especially since he was the only boy in the Idenbirken family. Leonardo returned his grandparents' love. He has fond memories of long walks in the beautiful countryside and exciting shopping expeditions in the city of Dusseldorf with his grandparents.

Undoubtedly his most ardent fan, Leonardo's mother, Irmelin, often accompanies her son to parties and ceremonies. Irmelin is also in charge of Leo's busy schedule.

Leonardo also received a unique gift from his visits with his German grandparents and from his mother's prompting—he learned to speak German at an early age. Irmelin continues to saturate him with her native culture. As he recently told a reporter, "She's always instilling European values in me, things about health, relaxation, exercise and food."

Leonardo was also very close to his stepbrother, Adam Starr, the son of George's second wife. Although the boys did not spend as much time together as they would have liked, they had a close relationship. In fact, it was Adam who spurred Leonardo's interest in acting, particularly the financial rewards. Although Leonardo appreciated the well-rounded lifestyle his parents gave him, he still hoped to earn enough money to improve his mother's modest financial means. Little did Leonardo realize that he would go from the ghettos of Hollywood to its most elite environment in such a short time.

Leonardo first encountered the monetary rewards of acting when Adam was cast in a Golden Grahams breakfast-cereal commercial. Adam's earnings for that small career step stimulated Leonardo's belief that maybe acting was the way he could fulfill those dreams he had for himself and his mother. "I asked my dad how much Adam made from it. He said, 'About $50,000.' $50,000! It just kept going through my head: My brother has $50,000! And that kept being my driving force. I just remember for, like, five years thinking my brother was better than me because he had that."

There was a twinge of jealousy when Adam landed a role in the television series *Battlestar Galactica*. But, in fact, Leonardo had been considering acting for several years. His interest had begun when he was a child and had avidly followed his favorite television show, *Romper Room*. Irmelin got him a spot on the show as one of the school children when he was five. After only one day, however, Leonardo was asked to leave. He became too disruptive, running and jumping on the set, and the crew could not control him.

It was not until nine years later that Leonardo decided to try acting once more. His parents supported him, taking him to his many auditions and interviews. He was turned down a number of times, often for trivial reasons such as his haircut or his name. After one such rejection he was devastated. "On the way home in the car I cried and said, 'Dad, I really want to become an actor, but if this is what it's about, I don't want to do it.' He put his arm around me and said, 'Someday, Leonardo, it will happen for you. Remember these words. Just relax.' And then I stopped crying, and I said, 'O.K.'"

At one point, an agent suggested he change his name to Lenny Williams so that it would be less ethnic. Leonardo, who has always been sensitive about his name, refused. He would not change it, even for a stage name. If Leonardo's name was a drawback, his physical characteristics were an advantage. He was a very attractive youngster, and he looked younger than his age. As a child actor these were important attributes. People want

Leonardo says that from early on, he loved to perform and always wanted to be an actor. Appearing on TV commercials was the first step in fulfilling his wish.

to see a good-looking child. And because he was older, he could memorize lines more readily, as well as follow directions more clearly.

Leonardo earned his first acting job at age 14 portraying a 10-year-old in a commercial for Matchbox toy cars and trucks. The Matchbox appearance led to roles in other commercials, some for toys, others for cereal or bubble gum. Leonardo did more than 30 commercials in all. While still doing commercials, he stepped into more "theatrical" roles, appearing in two educational films, *Mickey's Safety Club* and *How to Deal with a Parent Who Takes Drugs.*

Soon, the young actor began to land roles in various television shows. Leonardo was delighted to briefly play a troubled teen on the TV series *Lassie.* "I did two episodes of *Lassie.* I remember just being all excited," Leonardo laughs. He also appeared on *Roseanne* and on the series version of *The Outsiders.* His character in *The Outsiders* was similar to his role in *Lassie.* In fact, he was quickly gaining a reputation for portraying troubled teens. Leonardo believed these were excellent roles to enhance his abilities and prove that he could be a dramatic actor. "I haven't played a cheerful boy yet. But portraying emotionally ill characters gives me the chance to really act," he said in 1990.

Although Leonardo appreciated these short-term roles, he still hoped to appear as a regular on a show. It happened, but temporarily, when he joined the daytime soap opera *Santa Barbara.* Again he was cast as a troubled character, a teenage alcoholic. Acting in the "soaps" was completely different from Leonardo's previous experience, and he found it much more demanding.

Every day he had to memorize a new script, often with numerous pages of dialogue to learn. "I had to memorize a lot of lines for the part," he said at the time, "and sometimes I had trouble. Everyone was real patient and when I messed up it wasn't that big a deal." Another challenge faced the 15-year-old actor, however. During his stint on *Santa Barbara*, Leonardo had to keep up with his schoolwork. Whenever he had a spare moment, he studied with an on-set tutor.

While building his acting skills on the soap opera, Leonardo had little time for a personal life. Despite his hectic schedule, he did meet a girl and have his very first date. It was not the romantic or mystical experience that most of Leonardo's fans would now expect. In fact, it was a rather disastrous first date. Leonardo recalls the experience: "My most devastating girlfriend was in junior high. We were totally in love, and we finally went out on a date to see *When Harry Met Sally.* . . . I was so uncomfortable. I remember her eating this French-dip sandwich and the only thing I knew how to do was make fun of her and she got all freaked out. She didn't talk to me for a long time."

Although Leonardo's love life lacked something, his career was moving ahead as he continued to land more roles. He gained valuable experience on *Santa Barbara*, but once his role was over, he decided not to do another soap. It was too demanding, and he wanted a regular weekly, not daily, show. Not long after, he got his opportunity. In fact, just as his role on *Santa Barbara* was ending, he won a part in an upcoming sitcom that would give his career an enormous boost.

3

"Sitcom Growing Gains"

Leonardo DiCaprio became Garry Buckman, another troubled teen trying to come to terms with his parents' divorce in the new half-hour sitcom *Parenthood*. A spin-off of the 1989 hit movie *Parenthood*, the show focused on the lives of modern-day families. With a combination of humor and drama, *Parenthood* intended to evoke a medley of emotions from viewers as they related to the trials and joys of the families.

For Leonardo, his role as Garry was at this point his most important move toward success as an actor. When he found out about the part, he knew he could play the role. He recalled the audition: "I was like really excited about it. I had seen the movie lots of times. I knew what the character was like, and knew I would be good at it. I tried out for it, and then I went on a callback. I was one of the final three. I really concentrated. I went in there and did my best, and I got the part."

Because it was a weekly show, Leonardo's face became more and more familiar, appearing regularly in teen magazines. Teenagers began to label him as the "hot new idol."

For young Leonardo, happiness was landing his first continuing role on a weekly TV series, Parenthood. *He enjoyed playing misfit Garry Buckman, claiming it gave him a chance to "really act."*

Unfortunately, however, his growing popularity could not keep the show going. *Parenthood* debuted on August 20, 1990, and received excellent reviews as "a series about family life complete with passion and conflict." But the last regular episode aired on December 16, less than four months later.

Leonardo's on-set education ended once again with the cancellation of *Parenthood.* It was back to a regular classroom. Although he attended The Center for Enriched Studies and John Marshall High School in Los Angeles, Leonardo was never thrilled with classrooms. He was a good student, but he did not like to learn in that atmosphere. "I was frustrated in school," he confesses. "I wasn't happy learning things. I know it's up to you to earn a degree, but a lot of times school is just so dull and boring, it's hard for a kid to learn in that environment. You go to school, you go to this class, study this, study that, get your homework, go home. There's hardly any vibrance there. I could never focus on things I didn't want to learn. I used to do break-dancing skits with my friend at lunchtime. I had this one science class where the teacher would give me ten minutes after the class ended and I would get up and do improv. I needed to go to a place where I was excited about what I was learning. For me, it's all about getting a person interested in a subject by linking a lot of happiness to it, a lot of joy in doing it. That was lacking for me—and maybe a lot of other kids in this country."

Like many child and teen actors, Leonardo played the class clown. He often pulled jokes and ridiculous antics to help enliven his days at school. Sometimes he went a bit too far as an actor. One day he arrived at school with a swastika painted on his forehead and proceeded to imitate notorious criminal Charles Manson. Although his classmates knew he was only being silly, his teachers were not amused. His father came to the school and convinced the authorities that Leonardo was not a demented teen but was only having some misguided fun. After much persuasion, his teachers eventually relaxed, but with the agreement that such behavior would not occur again. There was little worry about that, however, for Leonardo would not remain long in a regular classroom.

Leonardo was about to get the chance to increase his popularity with television viewers. The successful sitcom *Growing Pains*, about a psychiatrist and his family, was in its seventh season. But the show was slipping in the ratings. Looking for a way to revive the sitcom, the producers decided to add a character whom teenagers could admire and relate to. And so, Luke Brower was created. Luke was a homeless boy who came to live with the Seaver family. Again, Leonardo portrayed a teenager in trouble, and his portrayal of Luke added immeasurably to his experience as an actor and won him some fans' hearts along the way.

Leonardo knew how to pull laughter from the audience with his hilarious antics and silly lines. He also tested his dramatic abilities with the character of Luke when he had to cry on cue. Although it was a little

Leonardo surprises Kirk Cameron in the sitcom Growing Pains. *Playing the disturbed but likable Luke Brower, Leonardo displayed his dramatic and comic talents and further enhanced his career.*

embarrassing at first, Leonardo quickly learned how to make the tears fall upon request. He admitted later that his secret was to imagine his mother in pain, and he would cry instantly.

Combining a troubled character with a comical personality was a rewarding experience for Leonardo. He admired Luke and believes that his portrayal was appropriate. "I liked the fact that he was homeless, yet it didn't really affect him," Leonardo explained. "He tried to cover it up, but his circumstances never affected him too much. He's a nice, charming guy who knows how to weasel his way out of things. . . . A street person isn't necessarily a bum or a depressed character. Luke gives people a more realistic image of someone in his position—he is witty, smart, and has a good sense of humor, just like anyone else!"

The role of Luke added new dimensions to Leonardo's acting experience. *Growing Pains* was filmed before a live studio audience. For an actor, this is comparable to performing on the stage. Leo explained how this type of filming worked.

"Monday, we come in and do a cold reading. We just read our scripts around the table, then we go in, and we start moving around with the script, on the sets, then we read with our script. Then the next day we are working on the set, rehearsing with our sides [individual script pages]. By the third day we should have it memorized, all of our lines. We block everything: where we are going to move, then we practice all day before showtime. We actually tape on Thursday, just in case there is a mess-up. It is pretty fun. More fun than filming every day. The hardest part is when the curtain goes up, and then you're really nervous."

The experience he gained in working with the other actors, who bonded immediately with Leonardo, was also very important. Included among the actors were Alan Thicke, Joanna Kerns, Tracey Gold, Jeremy Miller, and Kirk Cameron, all established players.

Leo enjoys clowning around with others on and off the set. His wit and charm immediately attract those around him.

There were initial fears that the introduction of Luke's character might cause some conflict among members of the cast, especially with Kirk Cameron. Kirk had enthralled teens for six years, and now Leonardo was trying to recapture that age group. The apprehension vanished once Leonardo arrived on the set. Much like their characters on the show, Leonardo and Kirk related well off the set.

Kirk helped Leonardo deal with his growing star status and popularity, and he held Leonardo in high regard. "He's coping very well," said Kirk. "We've had long talks about it. One day we walked outside the studio, and some fans came up to us. We signed autographs and kept walking. He's done very well, and he's being bombarded. I told him to have fun with it. I was always very grateful to the fans, and so is he. He's getting a lot of fan mail and is trying his best to answer it all."

Leonardo was gaining a steady following through *Growing Pains*. But it was not enough to improve the show's ratings, and it was dropped after its seventh season. Among the producers, however, Leonardo's rating was very positive. They discussed a spin-off starring Leonardo's character, but the idea was never realized. Although breaking up the cast was sad for Leonardo, he was already taking a bold jump in his career. In fact, he had been excused from the last few episodes of *Growing Pains* to concentrate on his first starring role on the big screen.

THIS BOY'S LIFE

Leonardo actually made his movie debut before appearing in *Growing Pains*. It was a film he prefers to forget. *Critters 3* was a low-budget horror movie, a second sequel to the original film. In it, Leo played the son of a slumlord. According to critics and viewers alike, *Critters 3* was a bomb that never should have been filmed. Although Leonardo's credibility as an actor did not suffer, he agreed. He removed the film from his credits.

Leo had also accepted a film role while working in *Growing Pains*. It was a minor part in the 1992 movie *Poison Ivy*, starring Drew Barrymore. The film was somewhat controversial because of the storyline, involving a sexual relationship between a teenage girl and a friend's father. Leo played "Guy #1," a role so small the character did not even warrant a name, and audiences could barely catch a glimpse of him. Although brief, these film appearances encouraged Leonardo to think more about furthering a film career.

But Leonardo's *real* movie debut was in *This Boy's Life*, and it was a spectacular beginning. While auditioning for the part of Tobias Wolff, Leonardo met one of his favorite actors, Robert De Niro, who played Tobias's stepfather. In

---

Leonardo's breakthrough came when he beat out hundreds of other young actors to play Robert De Niro's abused stepson in This Boy's Life *in 1993.*

the audition with De Niro, Leonardo felt intimidated by the respected older actor. But he did not let his fears show. Leonardo recalls, "It was overwhelming to meet Mr. De Niro. But I tried not to think about it. I just went in and played the part. I was confident, even though I had never done anything like it before. Now I realize it was ignorant confidence."

Ignorant confidence worked. Leonardo's performance was incredible. In fact, he was one of the first actors to audition, and the director, Michael Caton-Jones, auditioned 400 other actors for the part, just to be sure. None of them came close to measuring up to Leo's performance. The director knew that Leo was perfect for the part.

This Boy's Life is based on the memoir of author Tobias Wolff. Set in 1957, it chronicles a young boy struggling to come to terms with his life. The film captures Tobias's conflict and turmoil in living with his abusive and cruel stepfather. Leonardo's performance in the movie received excellent reviews from critics, audiences, and his fellow cast and crew. The director was no exception: "I have three excellent actors in this film, especially Leonardo. He is the rock that this movie is built on. If people can't relate to the character of Toby, the story becomes voyeuristic, but Leonardo makes this kid's struggle something you can connect with immediately." The Los Angeles Film Association agreed, giving Leonardo the New Generation Award for his role.

This Boy's Life, though not a blockbuster film, gave Leonardo a strong foundation on which to build his movie career. He did not hesitate. While finishing his role as Tobias, he

received another film offer, one that was to become the most important to date for the young actor. The film was *What's Eating Gilbert Grape*, the story of a young man who feels trapped in a small town in Iowa. Played by Johnny Depp, Gilbert takes care of his dysfunctional family, which includes his brother Arnie, a 10-year-old mentally disabled boy, Leonardo's character. Gilbert's 500-pound mother has not been out of the house in seven years, Arnie's behavior is generally foolish and dangerous, and Gilbert's sisters fight endlessly.

Could a 19-year-old actor portray a mentally disabled 10-year-old boy? Leonardo could and did when he played Arnie in What's Eating Gilbert Grape. *He received accolades from viewers and critics and recognition from the film industry with an Oscar nomination for Best Supporting Actor.*

What's Eating Gilbert Grape is an extraordinary story about unhappiness and disappointment as well as the fun and hope life can bring to one family. Johnny and Leonardo played their contrasting characters with a natural ease. The two actors enjoyed working together and formed a warm friendship. Leo credited Johnny's accurate portrayal of Gilbert with helping him play the intense role of Arnie so well. Still, it was Leonardo who received the attention and praise for his portrayal of Arnie.

It was well-deserved praise. Leonardo invested a considerable amount of time studying and working with mentally challenged children to understand Arnie's character. He watched numerous video tapes and traveled to Texas to spend a few days at a home for mentally disabled teenagers. Leonardo felt that portraying Arnie gave him an opportunity to show people that mentally disabled children should not be stereotyped. "People have these expectations that retarded children are really crazy and 'out there,'" says Leonardo. "But it's refreshing to see them. Everything is new to them."

To bring his character to life, Leonardo tried to forget everything about the characters in his previous roles and concentrated on Arnie's traits and actions. Arnie was very different from other characters Leonardo had played and also very different from Leonardo. In fact, the director, Lasse Hallström, wasn't sure that Leonardo was right for the part. Hallström worried that Leonardo's handsome features would detract from Arnie's disabilities. But

Leonardo proved looks did not matter. He could connect with the character.

His Arnie was annoying and reckless, but he was also charming and sweet. His free spirit delighted viewers, even if they were distressed by his heedless antics.

It was not only viewers who raved about Arnie. Critics were ecstatic. *The Washington Post* wrote, "DiCaprio's characterization of Arnie is a startling tour de force, a marvelous, completely unself-conscious performance." Another critic wrote, "As Arnie, DiCaprio is nothing short of extraordinary. Though the film verges on worship of the retarded—Arnie is the most loving character in the film—he is also weird, embarrassing, and infuriating, and DiCaprio's body language is extremely accurate." And *Movieline* magazine revealed, "DiCaprio, who also won acclaim in last year's *This Boy's Life*, does the best retarded character I've ever seen in a movie. He does what Dustin Hoffman *thought* he was doing in *Rain Man.*"

Leonardo was rewarded for his role with an Academy Award nomination for Best Supporting Actor in 1994, placing him among such notables as Ralph Fiennes, Tommy Lee Jones, John Malkovich, and Pete Postlethwaite. Although happy to join his fellow actors, Leonardo was also nervous. He performs effortlessly in front of the camera but is extremely shy when confronted with a large group, particularly of his peers. Waiting for the winner to be called was for Leonardo a terrifying experience. "The Academy Awards was a big burden for me, because of my problem

Emotional scenes like this one, with Johnny Depp as Gilbert, led to Leonardo's Academy Award nomination. When told he had a pretty good chance of winning, Leonardo says he became a nervous wreck.

of speaking in front of big audiences," he claims. "I'm doing a lot better with it now, but it was just this gut-wrenching fear of slipping up and doing something horrible. . . ." When Tommy Lee Jones was announced as the winner, Leonardo was relieved rather than disappointed. He recalls his anxiety, "When they announced Tommy Lee Jones had won, I wanted to get down on the ground and thank God. Nobody was happier for him than me, that's the truth."

Just before Leonardo received the role in *What's Eating Gilbert Grape*, he had been offered a part in a film with Bette Midler called *Hocus Pocus*. He turned it down, deciding he would only do films with quality scripts and with roles he truly believed in. Unfortunately, he missed out on a role he was eager to play, that of the interviewer Malloy in *Interview with the Vampire*. River Phoenix, Leonardo's idol, was cast in the role. Although they had never met personally, Leonardo recalled one social encounter with River. "I was at a Halloween party . . . [in 1993] and I remember it was really dark and everyone was drunk and I was passing through these crowds of people so thick it was almost two lanes of traffic, when I glanced at a guy in a mask and suddenly knew it was River Phoenix. I wanted to reach out and say 'hello' because he was this great mystery and we'd never met, and I thought he probably wouldn't blow me off because I'd done stuff by then that was maybe worth watching. But then I got caught in a lane of traffic and slid right past him. The next thing I knew, River had died. That same night."

With River's untimely death, his role as Malloy was available, and Leonardo voiced his desire for the part. But the producers felt he was too young, and they cast Christian Slater in the role. Leonardo felt his first blast of rejection from the silver screen industry. Although rejected, Leonardo remained undaunted. And why should he be? This was only one rejection amid a shower of other possibilities. Leonardo just needed to find a movie that he believed in, as well as one whose cast believed in him.

5

ALWAYS A TROUBLED KID

The Foot Shooting Party was 22 minutes long and appeared only briefly in art house theaters. Leonardo played the lead role, that of a rock singer in the early 1970s. Upon receiving his draft notice, he shoots himself in the foot to avoid going to Vietnam. Although the film went unnoticed by most of the general public, Leonardo felt it offered a good opportunity. He also had a chance to have fun by dressing up in outrageous '70s outfits, wearing bell-bottoms and blond hair extensions. In fact, it would be hard to recognize Leonardo in this short film.

Leonardo kept the gun theme with his next film, only this time he had no trouble pulling the trigger. He did, however, have to be talked into playing the role of "the Kid" in the movie *The Quick and the Dead*. As a Western, it was not a film that he really wanted to be part of. Through the persistence of Sharon Stone, the lead, he eventually gave in. Stone had seen Leonardo's work and knew that he would be perfect for the part. "It was honestly not my idea of the type of movie I wanted to do next," he says. "I really had to think it through for a long time."

In The Basketball Diaries, *Leonardo played Jim Carroll, the real-life basketball star who struggled with drug addiction. Although another "troubled youth" role for Leonardo, it was his first starring role in a feature film, and he displayed an impressive dramatic ability.*

The movie's theme is typical of the Western that weeds out the fastest draw. The story centers around the Kid's father, played by Gene Hackman, and an annual quick-draw competition. Challengers draw on each other, and the one left alive gets a cash prize. Enter Stone's character, out for revenge on Hackman for killing her father. The Kid, unsuccessful in gaining his father's respect, turns vengeful and bitter. He also tries to woo Stone and enters the competition to win her attention. He is killed by his father.

Leonardo described his character this way: "I see the Kid as a good version of Billy the Kid. My character is somebody who is so completely insecure in himself that he has to put on a show to dazzle everybody, and that, to me, was very interesting. He develops this thing about being cool. He is only afraid of his father. He's cocky and confident until he gets around his father. Then he just begs for attention by trying to prove he can kill faster and better than any-one else in town. He's a sad case but a really interesting character to play."

The Quick and the Dead was not a hit in the theaters or with most of the critics. Stone and Hackman did not receive rave reviews. Leonardo, however, was praised for his per-formance and emerged from the experience unscathed.

Leonardo did not hesitate to consider his next role. When he received the script of *The Basketball Diaries,* he could not stop reading it. For years, other young actors had wanted to play the leading role of Jim Carroll, but his memoirs of his school years had yet to be filmed. Throughout the late 1980s, when studios

considered making the book a movie, President Ronald Reagan was attacking the adolescent drug problem and pushing his wife's "Just Say No" crusade. Because of the story line of *The Basketball Diaries*, studios were reluctant to turn Carroll's life into a film.

By 1995, the time seemed right, and Leonardo seemed right for the lead as the high-school basketball star who got involved with drugs. Leonardo had to do a lot of homework before he could adequately portray Jim Carroll and the effects of his drug abuse. The young actor's superb performance led to rumors that Leonardo was taking drugs on the set. They were only rumors. Rather, Leonardo spent many hours with a drug counselor to understand the full effects of certain drugs.

Leonardo (here with Gene Hackman) had misgivings about playing "the Kid" in The Quick and the Dead. *But he received good reviews, and it was another showcase film for his growing talent as a serious actor.*

Leonardo and a friend stroll along a street in New York City, where the press appeared to scold him for his "club-hopping" and hinted he was following in the tragic footsteps of River Phoenix. Leonardo's friends dismiss such concerns, noting that he is a very shrewd young man who is not about to do anything that will harm his career.

He knew the basics, but he depended upon the counselor to learn the behaviors associated with drug abuse. Leonardo also had to learn to become a skilled basketball player to explore the character and soul of Jim Carroll.

Leonardo's character begins as the school hunk and basketball star, envied for his looks and talent. But his descent from drugs for "fun" to drugs just to survive is swift and devastating. Leonardo's role was one of his most difficult. He fully captures the horrors of Carroll's dark and destructive world, and continues to breathe life into the character until the end when Carroll is finally on the road to recovery.

Unfortunately, Leonardo's incredibly accurate portrayal of Jim Carroll was not enough to make *The Basketball Diaries* a success. It did become somewhat of a cult film, but mainstream audiences did not take to the film, and it had a short run in theaters. Still, it was Leonardo's first starring role in a feature film. He also formed a close friendship with Mark "Marky Mark" Wahlberg, one of his costars. In fact, reporters suggested that Leonardo and Mark enjoyed life a little too much during the filming. They were often seen in the New York bars partying throughout the night. The press labeled Leonardo as a "party animal"—an image that seems to have remained with him ever since.

Leonardo also liked working on the East Coast, particularly in New York. "I love New York. I want to move here," he said during the production. "You could sit at one corner all day and probably have a more fulfilling day than traveling all over L.A. and seeing all the sights."

Perhaps because of his wild side off the set, Leo was offered the starring role in a Warner Brothers film about the life of James Dean. He turned it down, deciding that the pressure and criticism would be overwhelming in portraying a person so well known and so unique as the late James Dean. Instead, Leonardo decided to take on the role of another rebel, the 19th-century poet Arthur Rimbaud, in the movie *Total Eclipse.*

Arthur Rimbaud is not widely known in the United States. In his native France, however, he is as famous as James Dean. Leonardo's role was his most controversial to date. The poet's eccentric and rebellious character likely drew

As Rimbaud, the self-destructive, homosexual French poet, Leonardo played his most controversial role. He took a risk because the flamboyant, rebellious life of the young poet intrigued him and presented a major challenge.

Leonardo to the part. The film centers around the homosexual relationship between young Rimbaud and an older poet, Paul Verlaine, who becomes Rimbaud's mentor. The relationship is intense and destructive, and in the end, Rimbaud is ruined at the age of 37.

Leonardo took a risk playing Rimbaud. Although his reviews focused mainly on his portrayal of a homosexual, critics were positive about his performance. Again, the film did not do well at the box office nor did it enhance his career. But Leonardo never seemed to worry much about that aspect; he wanted to do films that were interesting. "I like the film for what it is," Leo says in the movie's defense. "If I had the opportunity to do it again, I would say yes, because it's such an interesting character to get to play. A lot of the time, real-life people can be a hundred times more interesting than any stories writers can create in their heads. And that character was one of the first rebels. He revolutionized poetry at the age of sixteen."

Leonardo was not reluctant to portray a gay character. When asked how he felt about playing sexual scenes with another man, Leonardo's reply was honest. "I don't have a problem with doing a film about a relationship of love with another man. That's just acting, you know what I mean? But as far as the kissing stuff, that's really hard for me, I'm not kidding. But I've faced the fact that I'm gonna have to do it, and I'm gonna do it because I supposedly love the guy. But the movie isn't about homo-sexuality, although I'm sure that's what the press is gonna be all over."

Leonardo was right—the press was all over it. Viewers often have difficulty separating actors from the characters they portray. Following *Total Eclipse*, rumors floated that he was gay or bisexual, and some of the gossip has continued throughout his megastar status since *Titanic*. But, if anything could change audiences' view about Leonardo's sexual orientation, it would be his next film, in which he played the most famous and hopeless romantic of all time.

6

ROMANTIC HERO

Leonardo was not sure about playing Shakespeare's Romeo, and he definitely was not playing him if it meant dressing in tights. With the lack of success of his previous few movies, Leonardo wanted to be very choosy in selecting another film. It must, he felt, be a film and a role that would advance his career. Redoing the Shakespearean play might not be the best move. Films about the ill-fated lovers Romeo and Juliet had been done before. None, however, were quite as unique as director Baz Luhrmann's modern day production of *William Shakespeare's Romeo + Juliet.*

Leonardo got the break he was looking for in *Romeo + Juliet.* It was a huge hit, particularly attracting the attention of teenagers. Based on the traditional story, this modern-day version presents a few new angles. Leonardo explained during an interview after the film was shot: "Our version seemed to me much more violent and much less romantic. . . . Violence was a big part of that world. It was a whole world of violence. The thing is it's now a world of guns and not swords."

The story is set not in Verona, Italy, as in the original,

Skepticism about Leonardo's ability to play the romantic hero Romeo was soon dispelled when the film Romeo + Juliet *opened. He and his costar, Claire Danes, heated up the screen with their passionate portrayal of the tormented young lovers.*

but rather in Verona Beach, Florida. The rival families do not chase one another on horseback. They careen around in modern transport, even sports cars. The famous balcony scene, during which Juliet calls for her lover in plaintive words, "O, Romeo, Romeo. Wherefore art thou Romeo?" now ends with a splash in the swimming pool. The storyline remains the same, however. Two young people indulge in a forbidden love and risk all, even death, to be together. And they still speak their lines in the Elizabethan English Shakespeare originally wrote.

Leonardo was still playing the role of a troubled teen, but this was his first part as a romantic hero, and he made quite an impression. It helped that his on-screen romance with Juliet, played by Claire Danes, was as passionate as Shakespeare had intended. Luhrmann recalls the attraction between the two young actors. "One thing that I have absolutely no doubt about in this film is their on-screen chemistry. It's the sort of thing that's so defined. You can have two fantastic actors and still, the moment you see them on screen, it's either there or it's not. They absolutely had it. And as it turned out, Leonardo and Claire were like brother and sister on the set." Others felt the couple's on-screen chemistry was so powerful because of a possible off-screen romance. However, Leonardo and Claire remained professional and kept their relationship strictly platonic.

The film was shot on location in Mexico City, and there were some difficult times. Many of the cast and crew, including Leo, came down with

Montezuma's revenge and spent several days recovering. Despite this, Leonardo was intrigued with Mexico and liked to go exploring. And he enjoyed the warm welcome he received from the Mexican girls who clamored to see him on the set.

Thanks to the film, Leonardo's popularity soared. He was a charming romantic hero. According to his fans, he fit the part perfectly, and he was becoming a Hollywood heartthrob. The film itself also affected many students, who began an active interest in Shakespearean literature. "I've had a lot of teachers tell me that it made their students get into Shakespeare for the first time," Leo boasts with delight. "It wasn't tedious to them anymore, and they wanted to read more."

Despite his initial reluctance, the star found his role as Romeo intensely satisfying. He reflects on his modern-day Romeo: "Well, it was an interesting character, once I really started to research him. Because you have this pre-planned idea of *Romeo & Juliet*, and what Romeo is supposed to be—just some fluffy, romantic type of guy. But then you realize he was a hopeless romantic, and then he meets Juliet. . . . He risks everything . . . his whole family, everything—and he marries this girl, which is such an honorable thing to do if you really believe in love like that, especially at that age. It's the ultimate love story. It's a masterpiece."

It was a masterpiece for Leonardo as well. *Romeo + Juliet* was number one at the box office the first weekend it opened, bringing in $12 million. It was the kind of film Leonardo needed to give him that push into stardom. He

Guns, not swords, were the weapons of choice in the modern version of Shakespeare's drama, as Leonardo's Romeo shoots his way out of trouble.

was not only being noticed by producers, directors, and critics, but now he was quickly becoming widely recognized by the general public. It was obvious from this film, as well as the later success of *Titanic*, that Leonardo fared well as the romantic hero. His audiences seemed to find this romantic-hero role the most natural and the most appropriate for the young, handsome actor.

Leonardo's next film would put him even more in the spotlight, especially since he costarred with such recognized names as Meryl Streep,

Diane Keaton, Gwen Verdon, and Hume Cronyn. He was also reunited with another actor from his past while working on *Marvin's Room*. Robert De Niro, who played a small part, coproduced the film. Leonardo obviously had left an impression on De Niro when playing opposite him in *This Boy's Life*, since De Niro suggested Leonardo for the part of Hank, the troubled son of Meryl Streep.

As the story begins, Lee (Meryl Streep) and Hank have been separated from their family for many years, only to be reunited when Lee's sister, Bessie (Diane Keaton), discovers she has leukemia and needs help. Lee and Bessie are contrasting personalities. Lee is the rebellious, selfish sister who took off in search of a better life while leaving Bessie to take care of their bedridden father. Bessie is the kind, gentle sister who shows Hank unconditional love for the first time.

Again, Leonardo's performance received rave reviews, and although his was not the starring role, he welcomed the opportunity to act with such star performers. "Meryl Streep is completely unlike any other actress I've ever worked with," he says, "just because I've never met anybody who could walk onto a set and— without saying anything—have complete and utter respect. I mean, everybody becomes silent when she walks in . . ." It was obvious, however, from the reaction of fans and the press to Leonardo's performance that he was pulling his own weight in the movie business.

Leonardo's personal life was becoming more and more public. Since he had been dubbed a heartthrob, his romantic life was of serious

*Leonardo escorted his then
private-life Juliet, model Kristin
Zang, to the premiere of* Romeo
+ Juliet. *A friend has noted
that Leonardo is "always with
one girl or another."*

interest. Rumors circulated that Leonardo was romantically involved with Alicia Silverstone, Sara Gilbert, and Juliette Lewis. Leonardo is quick to retort, however, that these relationships have been blown way out of proportion because the women are merely close friends. Leonardo has, however, dated model Kristen Zang for about fifteen months, which to date has been his longest romantic relationship.

Although he has been linked to several beautiful women, Leonardo says that he is not all that concerned about looks when it comes to the opposite sex, and although he might not be as romantic as Romeo, or even Jack Dawson, he is a romantic at heart. "I am the kind of guy who finds out what a girl likes and compliments them," says Leonardo, who enjoys taking long walks on the beach with the one he loves. "I like girls who are intelligent," he says. "Someone funny and pretty—with a nice personality . . . You've got to keep the faith. Who doesn't like the idea that you could see someone tomorrow and she could be the love of your life? It's very romantic."

But Leonardo is not looking too hard right now to find that perfect someone. He is too busy with his career to spend the time he feels is necessary on a serious relationship. "I definitely want to have the security of settling down someday. I'm looking forward to getting married and having kids," he confesses. "But it's not my time to do that right now." Since *Titanic*, Leonardo has not had much of a chance to get used to all the fame he has received from the film. In fact, he was already in the midst of shooting another movie when *Titanic* was released.

7

UNSINKABLE FAME

Before *Titanic* was released, Leonardo was starring, actually twice starring, in another film. He joined veteran actors Jeremy Irons, John Malkovich, Gerard Depardieu, and Gabriel Byrne in the 17th-century adventure *The Man in the Iron Mask*. With France as the setting, Leonardo plays the role of the cruel King Louis XIV, as well as that of the king's twin brother, Philippe. Imprisoned and locked into an iron mask, Philippe is the good brother who must be rescued so that France can be saved.

Leonardo was nervous at first being surrounded by such famous stars. But his costars made him feel welcome and put him at ease. *The Man in the Iron Mask* did fairly well at the box office. Worldwide it pulled in more than $140 million, which is not considered a flop by any means but is significantly less money than most so-called block-buster films make. Despite the rather negative reviews of the film, Leonardo generally garnered words of praise for his excellent performance in the dual role.

Before *Titanic* was released, Leonardo appeared in the film *Don's Plum*. He joined the cast as a favor to his friend,

---

Leonardo's status as a superstar was firmly established with Titanic. *It is not likely to be diminished even though his subsequent film,* The Man in the Iron Mask, *was not a huge success. Leonardo does not appear worried as he contemplates his future career.*

R. D. Robb, an aspiring director. The film start-ed out as a short story about people sitting around in a diner complaining about their lives. Leonardo agreed to help his friend as long the film would be a short flick. After shooting, however, Robb decided to enlarge the film into a full feature because he liked the film and because Leonardo's fame skyrocket-ed after the release of *Titanic. Don's Plum* still has not been released. Leonardo opposed releasing it as a feature film, and so it remains in limbo as Robb and Leonardo work out their dispute, possibly in court. It is also possible that this film may never hit theaters.

In addition to *Don's Plum,* there are other images of Leonardo which may never be seen by the general public. It is true his pictures appear in just about every magazine since his success in *Titanic,* including *Playgirl.* However, contrary to the original announcement of his nudity, Leonardo is fully clothed in the July 1998 issue of the risqué publication. He got involved in a lawsuit with *Playgirl's* publishers when they planned to show nude photos. Reportedly, the pictures included full-frontal nudity. Although the origin of the photos was never released, rumors surfaced that they were taken during the filming of *Total Eclipse.*

The lawsuit was settled after Leonardo's lawyer indicated that publishing the photos would be an "invasion of privacy" and would cause "emotional distress" because of the "offensive and objectionable" nature of the pic-tures and the fact that "a reasonable person of ordinary sensibilities would not want to dis-close in a nationally published magazine . . . his completely naked body."

Since *The Man in the Iron Mask*, Leonardo has taken some time off to relax and travel. Although he has considered directing or maybe producing a film in the future, for now he is content to stick with acting. However, Leonardo feels that he must be especially careful about which roles he accepts. He has seen wrong choices hurt the careers of others. "There are people who have gotten good roles at my age, and their careers later slowly sloped down. Meaning no disrespect to anybody, but I want to avoid that by holding out for high quality projects."

Leonardo filmed a cameo role in a Woody Allen film called *Celebrity* in 1998. As with many Allen films, little information was given about the film or Leo's role in it, except that he would possibly play a rock star who gets mobbed wherever he goes.

Another project reportedly in Leonardo's future is *Slay the Dreamer*, about the assassination of Martin Luther King Jr., in which it is reported he may portray Jeffrey Jenkins, a Southern lawyer. After *Titanic* Leonardo was connected to a number of other films, but nothing had been officially announced by the summer of 1998.

One role that many of Leonardo's fans, as well as his peers, would like to see him play is that of James Dean, even though the idea did not pan out earlier. "I think it's going to happen," Leonardo says. "But the script has to be great. It could be a year. It could be never, but it would be really interesting to get inside an actor. It would be an actor playing an actor. It could be a little tricky. You can never really *BE* him. You're always imitating him."

Boisterous and adoring fans flocked to the premiere of The Man in the Iron Mask *to get another look at their idol, Hollywood's hottest young star, Leonardo DiCaprio.*

So for now, Leonardo is waiting. He is waiting for the right film and role to come along. He is also waiting for the right woman to enter his life. In the meantime, Leonardo will enjoy life while he's not working. Even without a movie to continually whet his fans' appetites, you can bet that he's still the hottest young star. As one reporter remarked, "If you're talking about teen girls worldwide, there is nothing, nothing that touches Leonardo DiCaprio. He's hotter than hot."

If you are ever doubtful, just surf the Internet, where more than 500 Leo-related websites can be found. Or go into any teenage girl's bedroom; you will be sure to find a shrine to Leonardo DiCaprio. Or, better yet, check out *People* Magazine's 1998 listing of the "50 Most Beautiful People in the World." Leonardo's blue-green eyes and blond hair grace the cover.

FILMOGRAPHY

1991   *Critters 3*

1992   *Poison Ivy*

1993   *This Boy's Life*
       What's Eating Gilbert Grape

1994   *The Foot Shooting Party*

1995   *The Quick and the Dead*
       The Basketball Diaries
       Total Eclipse

1996   *William Shakespeare's Romeo + Juliet*
       Marvin's Room

1997   *Titanic*

1998   *The Man in the Iron Mask*
       Celebrity

TELEVISION APPEARANCES

1980   *Romper Room*

1987–88   *Mickey's Safety Club* (Educational Film)
          How to Deal with a Parent Who Takes Drugs (Educational Film)

1988   *Lassie* (guest appearance)
          The Outsiders (guest appearance)

1989   *Santa Barbara*
          A Circus Fantasy (guest appearance)
          Roseanne (guest appearance)

1990   *Parenthood*

1991–92   *Growing Pains*

CHRONOLOGY

1974   Leonardo Wilhelm DiCaprio is born on November 11 in Los Angeles.

1975   Parents, George DiCaprio and Irmelin Idenbirken, divorce.

1980   Makes his first television appearance on *Romper Room.*

1980s   Performs in various television commercials.

1991–92   Portrays Luke Brower in television sitcom *Growing Pains.*

1990s   Attends The Center for Enriched Studies and John Marshall High School in Los Angeles.

1993   Stars in his first feature film, *This Boy's Life,* with Robert De Niro and Ellen Barkin.

1994   Nominated for both an Academy Award and a Golden Globe Award for *What's Eating Gilbert Grape* (Best Supporting Actor).

1996   Costars with Claire Danes in *William Shakespeare's Romeo + Juliet.*

1997   Moves out of his mother's home and into his own home in Los Angeles; costars with Kate Winslet in *Titanic;* nominated for a Golden Globe Award for Best Actor (Drama) for his performance in *Titanic.*

1998   Plays a dual role in *The Man in the Iron Mask;* films Woody Allen's *Celebrity.*

AWARDS

1993   New Generation Award from Los Angeles Film Critics Association for *This Boy's Life;* Most Promising Actor from the Chicago Film Critics for *This Boy's Life;* runner-up for Best Supporting Actor from New York Film Critics Association and the National Society of Film Critics for *This Boy's Life.*

1994   Most Promising Actor from the Chicago Film Critics for *What's Eating Gilbert Grape;* Academy Award nomination for *What's Eating Gilbert Grape;* Golden Globe nomination for *What's Eating Gilbert Grape;* Best Supporting Actor Award from the National Board of Review for *What's Eating Gilbert Grape;* New Generation Award from Los Angeles Film Critics Association for *What's Eating Gilbert Grape.*

1996   Favorite Romance Actor Blockbuster Awards for *William Shakespeare's Romeo + Juliet;* Silver Bear Award for Best Actor in *William Shakespeare's Romeo + Juliet* from 47th Berlin International Film Festival; Golden Samovar Award in the Moscow Film Festival for *Marvin's Room.*

1997   Golden Globe nomination for Best Actor (Drama) in *Titanic.*

FURTHER READING

Bego, Mark. *Leonardo DiCaprio: Romantic Hero.* Kansas City: Andrews McMeel Publishing, 1998.

Catalano, Grace. *Leonardo DiCaprio: Modern Day Romeo.* New York: Bantam Doubleday Dell Publishing Group, Inc., 1998.

Garrard, Cathy. "Everything Leo: His Top Secrets Revealed." *Young and Modern,* May 1998.

Krulik, Nancy. *Leonardo DiCaprio: A Biography.* New York: Pocket Books, 1998.

"Leo DiCaprio: Thru The Years." *Teen Machine,* August 1998.

LFP Presents: Leonardo. Volume 3, Number 2, Beverly Hills: L.F.P., Inc., 1998.

"Our Fabulous 50." *People,* May 11, 1998.

Schindehette, Susan. "Full Speed Ahead!" *People,* April 20, 1998.

Tresniowski, Alex. "Leo's New Life." *Teen People,* May 1998.

Wells, Jeffrey, Joanna Blonska, and Jason Lynch. "The Love Boat." *People,* March 1998.

ABOUT THE AUTHOR

Stacey Stauffer has a degree in English and a concentration in creative writing and communications from Ursinus College in Collegeville, Pennsylvania. Several of her poems and short stories have been published in literary magazines, and her articles have been printed in local publications including the *Chester County Press* and a multicultural newspaper, *La Voz.* This is her second book published by Chelsea House. She has worked as a journalist, freelance writer and editor, and currently works in the sales and marketing department at Chelsea House Publishers.

INDEX

PHOTO CREDITS:
Paramount Picture/Photofest: 2; AP/Wide World Photos: 6, 10, 15; Reuters/ Ho/Archive Photos: 12; Darlene Hammond/Archive Photos: 16, 22, 24, 30; Gregg De Guire/London Features Int'l, Ltd.: 19; Archive Photos: 28, 46; Photofest: 32, 35, 40; Fotos Int'l/Archive Photos: 38, 48, 52; TriStar Pictures/ Photofest: 43; Freddy Baez/UFB/London Features Int'l, Ltd.: 44; Reuters/ Fred Prouser/Archive Photos: 54; Colin Mason/London Features Int'l, Ltd.: 56; Nick Elgar/UNE/London Features Int'l, Ltd.: 60.